CURRENT SCIENCE®

Meltdown!

Global Warming Puts the World on Thin Ice

By John Perritano

Reading Adviser: Cecilia Minden-Cupp, Ph.D., Literacy Consultant
Science Curriculum Content Consultant: Debra Voege, M.A.

Gareth Stevens
Publishing

Please visit our web site at www.garethstevens.com.
For a free color catalog describing Gareth Stevens Publishing's list of
high-quality books, call 1-800-542-2595 (USA) or 1-800-387-3178 (Canada).
Gareth Stevens Publishing's fax: 1-877-542-2596

Library of Congress Cataloging-in-Publication Data

Perritano, John.
    Meltdown! : global warming puts the world on thin ice / by John Perritano ;
    reading specialist, Cecilia Minden-Cupp ; science curriculum content
    consultant, Debra Voege.
        p. cm. — (Current science)
    Includes bibliographical references and index.
    ISBN-10: 1-4339-2240-1   ISBN-13: 978-1-4339-2240-4 (lib. bdg.)
    1. Global warming—Juvenile literature.   2. Global temperature changes—
Juvenile literature.   I. Title.
QC981.8.G56P47   2010
551.6—dc22   2009002273

This edition first published in 2010 by
Gareth Stevens Publishing
A Weekly Reader® Company
1 Reader's Digest Road
Pleasantville, NY 10570-7000 USA

Copyright © 2010 by Gareth Stevens, Inc.

Current Science™ is a trademark of Weekly Reader Corporation. Used under license.

Gareth Stevens Executive Managing Editor: Lisa M. Herrington
Gareth Stevens Senior Editor: Barbara Bakowski
Gareth Stevens Cover Designer: Keith Plechaty

Created by **Q2AMedia**
Editor: Jessica Cohn
Art Director: Rahul Dhiman
Designer: Harleen Mehta
Photo Researcher: Kamal Kumar
Illustrators: Ashish Tanwar, Indranil Ganguly, Priyanka Bajaj

Photo credits (t = top; b = bottom; c = center; l = left; r = right):
Norbert Rosing/Getty Images: cover, Q2AMedia Picture Bank: title page, Jan Martin Will/Shutterstock: 4,
Jan Will/Fotolia: 5, Q2AMedia Picture Bank: 6, Kurhan/Dreamstime: 7t, Jan Will Fotografie/Istockphoto: 7b,
Tim Boyle/Staff/Getty Images: 8, Nagy Melinda/Shutterstock: 9, SV Lumagraphica/Shutterstock: 12,
Daniel Stein/Istockphoto: 14-15, Shoot/Zefa/Corbis: 16, Konstantin Baskakov/Shutterstock: 17,
Hulton Archive/Stringer/Getty Images: 20, MJ Kim/Staff/Getty Images: 21, George Spade/Shutterstock: 22,
Kevin Fleming/Corbis: 23, Diana Haecker/Associated Press: 24, Dmitrijs Bindemanis/Shutterstock: 25,
John Gaps III/Associated Press: 26, Lyudmila Rudyuk/Fotolia: 27, Warren Faidley/Corbis: 28, Marc van
Vuren/Shutterstock: 29, NASA: 30, NASA/JPL: 31t, Steven Clevenger/Corbis: 32, OAR/ERL/National
Severe Storms Laboratory (NSSL): 32-33, Scott Olson/Contributor/Hulton Archive/Getty Images: 34,
Walter Bibikow/The Image Bank/Getty Images: 35, Laski Diffusion/Contributor/Getty Images: 36, Dark
O/Shutterstock: 37, Rafa Irusta/ Shutterstock: 38, Oorka/Shutterstock: 40, Tesla Motors: 41, Binod
Joshi/Associated Press: 42tr, Maica/Istockphoto: 42-43, David H Bromwich: 44, Rita Januskeviciute/
Shutterstock: 47
Q2AMedia Art Bank: 10-11, 13t, 13b, 18-19, 21br, 39

Printed in the United States of America
1 2 3 4 5 6 7 8 9 12 11 10 09

CONTENTS

Words in **boldface** type are defined in the glossary.

Chapter 1

A Global
WARMING

What could be cooler than polar bears? Polar bears live and hunt in the Arctic. They dive into ice-cold water. They loaf on Arctic ice. The big bears chase seals across sea ice. These kings and queens of cool are in trouble, however. Earth is warming up.

Ships can now plow through the once-frozen Arctic Ocean.

BEARS IN DANGER

Polar bears need sea ice. The bears are better at catching seals on ice than in water. The ice gives the bears a place to rest, too. Polar bears can swim 100 miles (161 kilometers) or more for food. Yet the distance between pieces of floating sea ice is getting greater. Melting sea ice has forced the bears to swim farther for dinner. As a result, bears are drowning at an alarming rate. About 25,000 polar bears remain in the wild. But they are in danger. **Global warming** is destroying their **habitat**. What is global warming? It is the steady increase of average temperatures across Earth.

GROUND ZERO

The Arctic is heating up at almost double the rate of the rest of the world. Arctic ice is thicker and wider in winter than in summer. The ice covers more area in March than in other months. Thirty years ago, ice covered half of the Arctic in March. In 2008, the ice covered less than 30 percent of the area in March.

FAST FACT
The loss of winter sea ice in the Arctic is equal to the area of Alaska, Texas, and Washington state combined!

BATTLEGROUND: ANTARCTICA

Antarctica is the world's coldest continent. Yet even the coldest place on Earth is warming up. In Antarctica, a small temperature increase makes a big difference. Melting Antarctic ice contributes to a rise in global sea levels of 0.08 inch (2 millimeters) a year.

THE BIG THAW

Antarctica's thick sheets of ice are thawing. These ice shelves are cracking and sliding into the ocean. In 1995, a chunk of ice broke off from the Larsen Ice Shelf. The chunk was half the size of Delaware. Three years later, 425 square miles (1,101 square km) of the Wilkins Ice Shelf crumbled. Four years after that,

Scientists say the Antarctic ice sheet is melting. Melting ice causes sea levels to rise.

another huge ice piece broke into icebergs. It had been frozen for 12,000 years.

THE PROBLEM WITH PENGUINS

Global warming is hurting Antarctica's **ecosystem**. Today, only about 200,000 pairs of emperor penguins live there. That is half the number of penguins counted 50 years ago. Warmer temperatures have also hurt **krill**, worsening the problem. Krill are the tiny shrimplike creatures that the emperor penguin eats.

Emperor penguins used to flourish in Antarctica. Their numbers are shrinking as global warming causes sea ice to melt.

A heat wave grips Chicago, Illinois. The last two decades were the hottest in 400 years.

SHEDDING LIGHT ON GLOBAL WARMING

How does global warming happen? Earth takes in **radiation** from the Sun. Some of the gases in Earth's **atmosphere** trap that radiation close to Earth's surface. The result is the **greenhouse effect**. A greenhouse takes in heat from the Sun and holds it. Earth takes in heat from the Sun to make life possible. Now, however, Earth is warmer than before.

FAST FACT
The world needs heat-trapping gases. Without them, temperatures would drop to 0 degrees Fahrenheit (-18 degrees Celsius). But researchers wonder if it is now too hot.

GREENHOUSE GASES

Scientists call the gases in the atmosphere **greenhouse gases**. The gases include **carbon dioxide** and **methane**. Most greenhouse gases occur naturally. Earth would freeze without them. Yet the burning of **fossil fuels** increases the greenhouse gases too much, many people say.

The burning of fossil fuels releases greenhouse gases into the air.

What are fossil fuels? They include oil, coal, and natural gas. These fuels are the remains of plants and animals that lived hundreds of millions of years ago. Over time, layers of rock built up over them. Time and the weight of the rock turned the once-living matter into fuels. These fuels can power machines, factories, and automobiles.

WHAT DO YOU THINK?

What are some ways people can reduce their need for fossil fuels?

GLOBAL WARMING AND THE GREENHOUSE EFFECT

Greenhouse gases such as carbon dioxide help create the greenhouse effect. The Sun's energy strikes Earth. It is quickly changed to heat energy. Plants, soil, and water take in some of that energy. A portion of the Sun's energy bounces back into space. However, heat-trapping gases such as carbon dioxide and methane keep the Sun's heat close to Earth's surface.

Radiation from the Sun passes through Earth's atmosphere.

Trapped energy

Released energy

The Sun's energy heats Earth's surface. Clouds, ice, and snow reflect some of that radiation into space.

Greenhouse gases trap the Sun's heat near Earth's surface, warming the planet. Too many greenhouse gases in the air results in global warming.

Chapter 2

Climate CLUES

Earth has gone through periods of natural cooling and heating. The planet was cold 2.4 billion years ago. Temperatures dropped below -90 degrees F (-68 degrees C). Then a thaw came. Extreme cold was followed by warmth five times in Earth's long history.

PAST AND PRESENT

A period of extreme cold is an **ice age**. The last ice age was about 18,000 years ago. Vast ice sheets covered the planet. Some of the **glaciers** were several miles or kilometers high. About 7,000 years ago, Earth began to warm. Ice melted. The oceans rose to today's level.

The Earth cooled again about 500 years ago. Scientists call this period the Little Ice Age. The planet warmed again afterward.

About 100 million years ago, the average temperature was actually about 18 degrees F (10 degrees C) warmer than it is today. So why are today's scientists sounding an alarm? Earth's temperature has increased more rapidly in the last 50 years. This increase happened as heat-trapping gases rose steadily.

Strange but True

The temperature on Venus is about 866 degrees F (464 degrees C). Scientists thought Venus was warm, but not that warm! Venus is closer to the Sun than Earth is. Yet scientists believed that the clouds on Venus shielded it from heat. What changed their minds? Scientists sent space vehicles to visit the planet. Researchers found that the surface of Venus is extremely hot. Lead, tin, and mercury would boil there.

Scientists also found that 97 percent of Venus's atmosphere is carbon dioxide. In other words, the greenhouse effect has turned Venus into one hot world! Life as we know it could not exist on Venus.

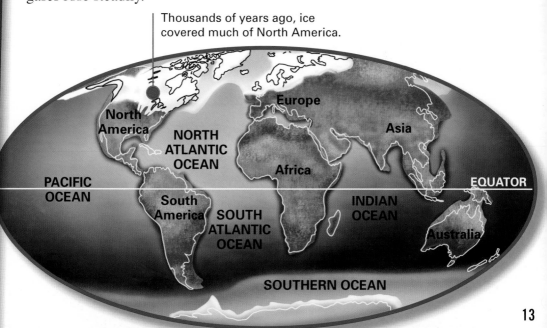

Thousands of years ago, ice covered much of North America.

North America

Europe

Asia

NORTH ATLANTIC OCEAN

Africa

PACIFIC OCEAN

EQUATOR

South America

SOUTH ATLANTIC OCEAN

INDIAN OCEAN

Australia

SOUTHERN OCEAN

13

ADDING GREENHOUSE GASES

Human activity increases heat-trapping gases in Earth's atmosphere. People add about 4.4 billion tons (4 billion metric tons) of carbon dioxide into the atmosphere each year. Over the last century, the increase in greenhouse gases has caused temperatures across the planet to increase nearly 1 degree F (0.6 degree C).

FAST FACT

The United States and Australia are two of the largest producers of carbon dioxide. Each country sends up to 36 billion tons (33 billion metric tons) of the greenhouse gas into the atmosphere each year.

HUMAN ACTIVITIES

Cars spit carbon dioxide into the air. Just turning on a light adds greenhouse gases, too. So does burning wood in a fireplace. Coal-burning factories contribute huge **emissions** of carbon dioxide. Trees take in some of that carbon dioxide and give off oxygen. Trees help reduce greenhouse gases. Yet loggers cut down vast stands of trees. Loggers in rain forests often burn the trees after cutting them down. Burning wood sends even more carbon dioxide into the air.

Some scientists say carbon dioxide emissions from all sources will rise to nearly 2.5 trillion tons (2.3 trillion metric tons). How soon? In less than 100 years!

Climate change is harming the air quality in many cities, including Los Angeles, California.

YOU DO IT!

Create Your Own Greenhouse Effect

What You Need
- two room thermometers
- clock or watch
- glass jar
- pad and pencil
- sunny area next to a window

What You Do
Step 1
Place the thermometers near the window. After four minutes, record the temperature on each thermometer.

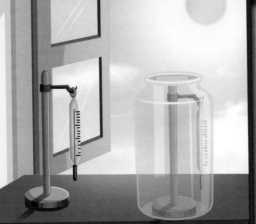

Step 2
Place the jar over one of the thermometers (or stand the thermometer in the jar). Keep the other thermometer exposed to the sunlight and air. Every minute, for 10 to 15 minutes, record the temperature on each thermometer. What can you conclude?

What Happened?
The air temperature in the jar was warmer than the air temperature outside the jar. The jar acted as a greenhouse.

SIGNS OF GLOBAL WARMING

You can see global warming in action. The increase in Earth's temperature is causing some rivers to dry up. Lack of rain is hurting crops. Some places are becoming too hot for certain animal and plant **species**. They move away or vanish. The heat creates conditions that lead to wildfires. The changes in weather encourage blizzards, floods, and hurricanes, too.

U.S. wildfires are on the rise. In the fall of 2008, record heat dried out land near Los Angeles, California. Strong winds gusted up to 75 miles (121 km) an hour. The winds fueled several wildfires. The fires burned through thousands of acres and destroyed almost 1,000 homes. Nearly 4,000 firefighters battled the blazes.

Wildfires are on the rise in the western United States.

FAST FACT

The Natonal Aeronautics and Space Administration (NASA) is studying the effects of forest fires on Arctic pollution. Satellites help researchers follow where the smoke blows.

Researchers say global warming is changing the length of the seasons.

HOW SWEET IT'S NOT!

Global warming has wide-reaching effects in the plant world. Maple syrup makers in New England say the sugaring season is starting earlier. This early start reduces the amount of sap tapped from maple trees. The syrup makers blame global warming.

SPRING FLOWERS

European scientists are studying flowers. They watch when the flowers bloom. The researchers have found that fall is ending later and spring is starting sooner. The scientists say the growing season is now 11 days longer because of climate change.

WHAT DO YOU THINK?

What other plants show signs of global weather changes? Think about what grows near your home.

Sharing the PROBLEM

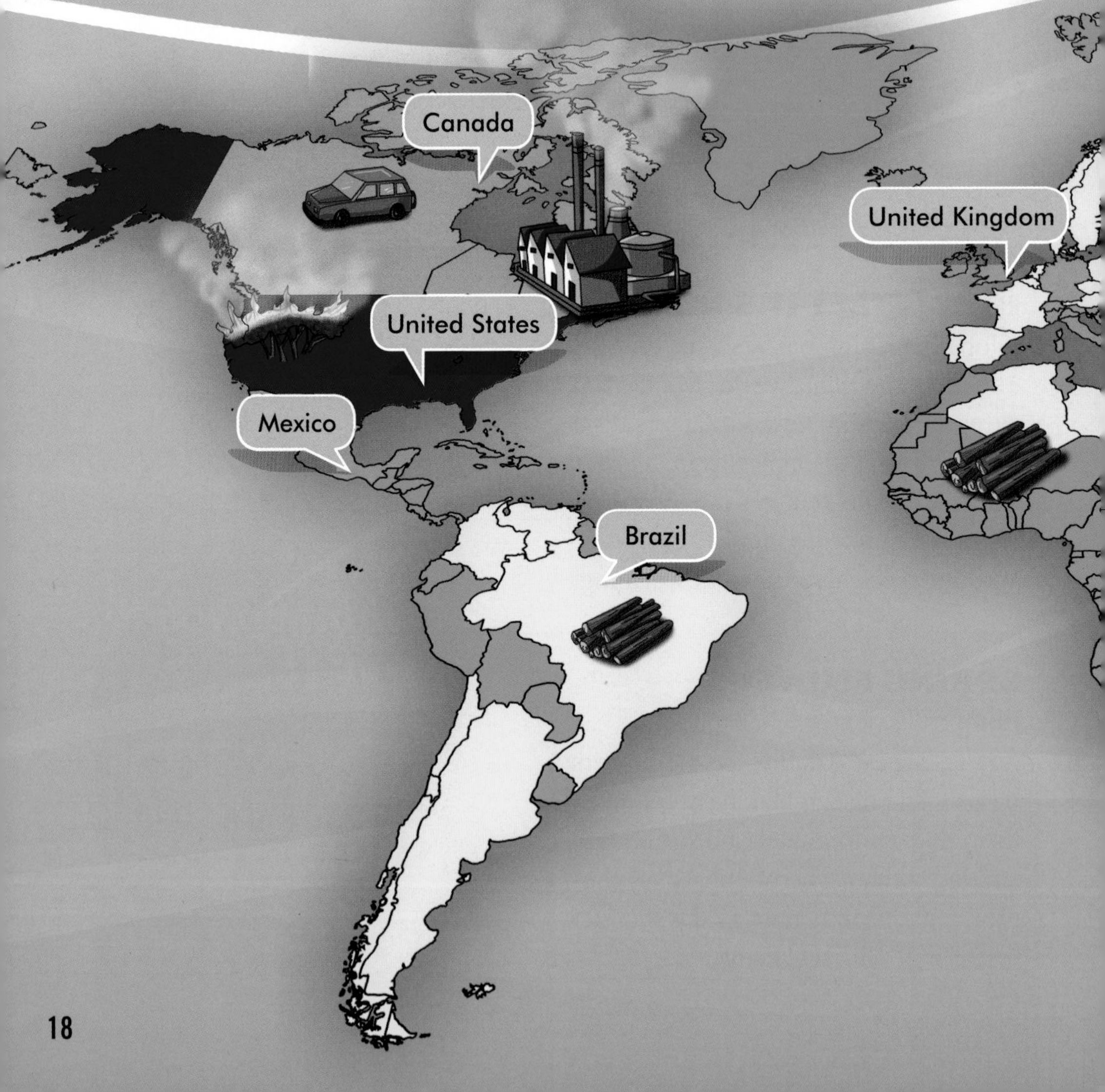

This world map shows the amount of carbon dioxide emissions by country. Carbon dioxide is released when people burn fossil fuels to heat homes, power factories, and run vehicles. The United States has only 5 percent of the world's population. But it emits about one-third of the world's greenhouse gases.

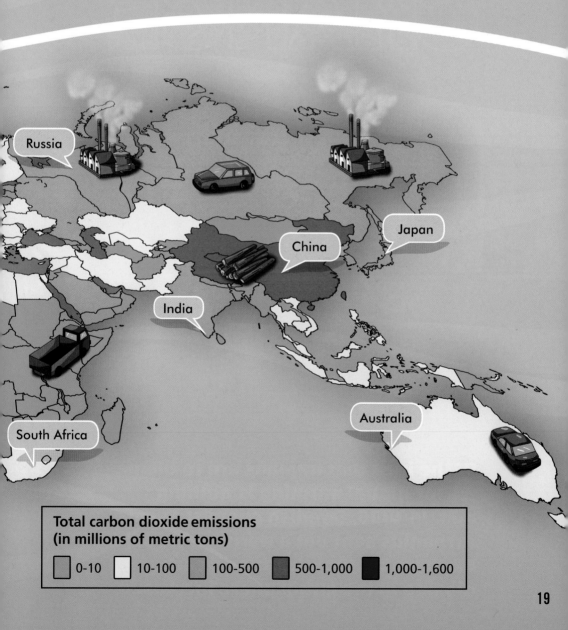

Total carbon dioxide emissions
(in millions of metric tons)

| 0-10 | 10-100 | 100-500 | 500-1,000 | 1,000-1,600 |

Chapter 3

The Science of Climate CHANGE

The idea that humans are to blame for global warming is nothing new. In 1896, Swedish chemist Svante Arrhenius sent out a warning. He said Earth would grow warmer if carbon dioxide in the atmosphere increased.

WORDS OF WARNING

No one paid much attention to Arrhenius until 1957. In that year, Roger Revelle and Hans Suess issued a warning. These climate scientists said the oceans could not absorb the extra carbon dioxide that was being made. They said a warmer planet would result.

TEMPERATURE RISING

After 1957, scientists began studying climate change more seriously. They looked at temperatures from the 1800s until now. They found that Earth's surface temperature rose by about 1 degree F (0.6 degree C). Most of that change occurred in the 1970s. Human activities contributed to a 20 to 30 percent increase in carbon dioxide.

In 2007, former U.S. Vice President Al Gore won the Nobel Peace Prize for his work on global warming. Gore wrote a book and made a movie called *An Inconvenient Truth*. The book and movie detail the problem of climate change.

The Carbon Cycle

Carbon enters the atmosphere through a process called the **carbon cycle**. Soil and rocks contain a lot of carbon. Ocean water and **sediments** contain vast amounts of carbon, too.

Released carbon combines with other elements. It forms **compounds** such as carbon dioxide. Plants take in carbon dioxide to make food, or sugar. Plants use that food to make seeds and leaves.

Animals and people eat plants as food. They release carbon dioxide as their bodies turn the food into energy they can use. When animals or plants die, they decay. That process puts carbon back into the environment.

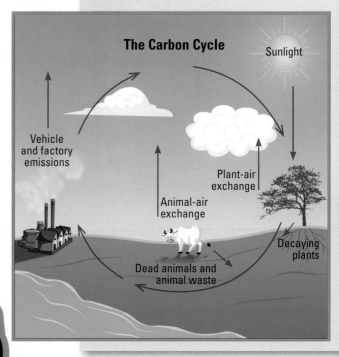

The Carbon Cycle

Sunlight

Vehicle and factory emissions

Plant-air exchange

Animal-air exchange

Decaying plants

Dead animals and animal waste

Former U.S. Vice President Al Gore has worked to help stop climate change.

21

OPPOSING VIEWS

The majority of scientists agree that global warming is real. They believe human activity is to blame. Other scientists are not so sure. Those scientists say the rise in temperature is part of a natural cycle.

Those who say warming is natural look to Antarctica to prove their point. Some ice sheets are indeed collapsing. Other ice sheets, however, are becoming thicker.

Some scientists say that the math used to figure out what will happen in the future is not the best math available. Almost all people, however, agree that the weather needs more study.

Thawing ice could open up areas for oil or natural gas drilling.

STAKING CLAIM

Some people believe that global warming might be good in some ways. Thawing ice could open new areas for oil exploration or natural gas drilling. A thaw could also mean more mining and fishing. In fact, some countries are already staking claim to what lies underneath the water.

Melting ice may create new fishing areas.

FAST FACT
Sea levels could rise 4 to 35 inches (10 to 89 centimeters) by the end of the century.

High seas are destroying the Alaskan town of Shishmaref.

HUMANS IN DANGER

People in Shishmaref, Alaska, know that global warming is real. Shishmaref is a tiny town on Sharichef Island. Sea ice once protected the small village from floods and waves. No longer! The lack of ice is destroying the community. It is forcing people to leave the island.

TROUBLE IN TUVALU

The tiny island of Tuvalu (too-VAH-loo) is having the same kind of trouble. In 50 years, the Pacific Ocean will swallow the island, whose area is only 10 square miles (26 square km). Many of the people from the island have already left.

What will happen if ice melt continues at this rate? In several hundred years, much of the East Coast of the United States may be underwater. Think of New York City underwater! In Europe, the Netherlands and other nations could also go under.

DISEASE ON THE RISE

Rising seas are one by-product of global warming. Disease is another. As Earth warms, disease-carrying insects, germs, and viruses increase. Many germs and viruses find it difficult to survive in the cold.

The number of disease-carrying insects has already risen. Diseases carried by mosquitoes are showing up in new areas. Near the equator, many countries are facing **epidemics**. Diseases such as malaria and cholera are increasing because of higher temperatures worldwide.

A warmer climate means more mosquitoes! The insects spread serious diseases, including malaria.

WHAT DO YOU THINK?

Which countries are most responsible for acting to stop global warming?

High temperatures and dry conditions turn fields into deserts.

IMPACT ON WILDLIFE AND PLANTS

Animals and plants are undergoing changes as the planet warms. The behavior of animals and plants relates to the environment.

Global warming has forced many animals to change their habits. For example, some bird species have altered their **migration** patterns. American robins are leaving their winter homes in the south for breeding areas in the north much earlier in the year. In winter, many birds stay farther north than they did before.

PLANKTON IN PERIL

While some animals are adapting, others are vanishing. Tiny **plankton** are at the bottom of the ocean food chain. Warmer waters do not supply the nutrients plankton need to survive. The plankton population is going down. This decrease has led to a drop in the number of fish that eat plankton. As a result, birds that eat the fish are also in danger.

EFFECTS ON PLANTS

The frozen Arctic **tundra** has been treeless. Now trees are slowly invading the tundra. Why? Global warming affects the growth of forests. To show how, scientists have built several pumping stations near a forest in North Carolina. The scientists constantly pump carbon dioxide into the air. Trees that are exposed to a constant rush of carbon dioxide are growing 25 percent faster than trees that are not exposed to the gas.

Global warming is affecting all the animals in the ocean food chain.

WHAT DO YOU THINK?

Are humans responsible for global warming? Why or why not?

Chapter 4

Wild WEATHER

Get out your umbrellas! Some scientists predict the planet will be hammered with more severe weather as Earth's temperature increases. There will be powerful hurricanes and snowstorms. People will experience disastrous heat waves.

Extreme weather can cause flooding that destroys people's homes.

WEATHER TO THE EXTREME

Why do some scientists relate extreme weather to global warming? Scientists say a warmer world means a wetter world. A wetter world means more intense storms. As heat increases, so does **evaporation**. As evaporation increases, so do the chances for more snow and rain. Weather patterns will also change. Winds will become stronger. **Droughts** will worsen. Snow, rain, and ice storms will become more intense.

YOU DO IT!

Make Rain

Be sure to have an adult help you with this activity.

What You Need
- large glass jar with a metal top
- hot tap water
- dinner plate
- ice cubes

What You Do

Step 1
Have the adult fill the jar with 2 to 3 inches (5 to 8 cm) of hot tap water.

Step 2
After one to two minutes, put the plate on top of the jar. Next, put the ice cubes on top of the plate. After about 15 minutes, you will see "rain" fall inside the jar.

What Happened?
The warm, moist air inside the jar reacted with the cold plate, forming water vapor. The vapor formed droplets that fell from the lid. That process is called **condensation**. It also happens in the atmosphere when warm, moist air rises and meets colder air. The vapor condenses, creating **precipitation**. Rain, sleet, and snow are forms of precipitation.

29

WEATHER CHANGES

El Niño and **La Niña** are periods when the ocean warms or cools. Some **climatologists** say these ocean events are connected to global warming. The events change weather patterns on land and at sea.

EL NIÑO

El Niño is the warming of the waters in the tropical Pacific Ocean. One of the strongest El Niños occurred in 1997 and 1998. In February 1997, scientists watched in amazement as El Niño took hold. Almost all the cold water near the equator disappeared.

The weather on land changed dramatically. El Niño was responsible for a severe drought in Indonesia. It happened between March and December. The islands usually receive 90 inches (229 cm) of rain during these months. Only half that amount fell. By July, it was so dry that wildfires burned out of control in Sumatra and Borneo.

Jet streams are bands of strong wind high above Earth. Many experts say global warming has shifted the jet streams. That shift could affect worldwide weather patterns.

Jet streams

Trade winds

Trade winds move along the equator. Researchers say global warming is weakening the trade winds in the Pacific Ocean.

LA NIÑA

La Niña brings cold water from the deep sea to the surface. Scientists blamed La Niña for many weather events, including U.S. droughts and hurricanes. They blamed the cooling for record snowfall and tornadoes in the 1990s.

This satellite image shows La Niña. The warmest ocean areas are shown in red.

The Conveyor Belt

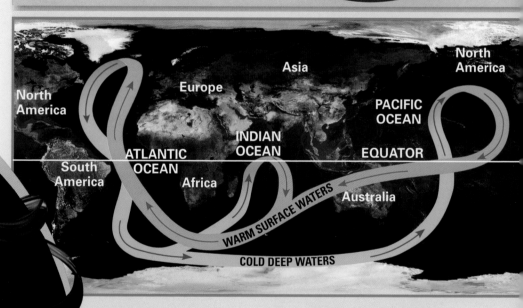

North America

Asia

Europe

North America

PACIFIC OCEAN

ATLANTIC OCEAN

INDIAN OCEAN

EQUATOR

South America

Africa

Australia

WARM SURFACE WATERS

COLD DEEP WATERS

El Niño and La Niña are not the only climate patterns scientists worry about. They are also concerned that global warming will shut down the "conveyor belt." That is a huge ocean current. This current carries warm surface waters toward the Poles and cold deep waters toward the equator.

The current has stopped in the past, say scientists. Freshwater from melting glaciers and an increase in precipitation could stop the belt again. If that happens, a harsh chill would hit the Northern Hemisphere. Droughts and other severe weather could occur elsewhere.

MIGHTY WINDS

From Texas to Cuba and from Mexico to Canada, the 2008 hurricane season was one for the record books. It was the most active in recent memory. A record number of storms struck the Atlantic coast. Five of the 16 storms were major hurricanes. Scientists at the National Oceanic and Atmospheric Administration said the season was unusually active. The temperature of the tropical Atlantic was 1 degree F (0.6 degree C) above normal.

STRONGER HURRICANES

Get used to the wind. As Earth's temperature increases, scientists say, hurricanes will become stronger. Warm air near the surface of the ocean fuels these storms. An ocean storm becomes a hurricane when winds reach at least 74 miles (119 km) an hour. Researchers at the Massachusetts Institute of Technology say that the intensity of hurricanes has grown by 50 percent over the past 30 years.

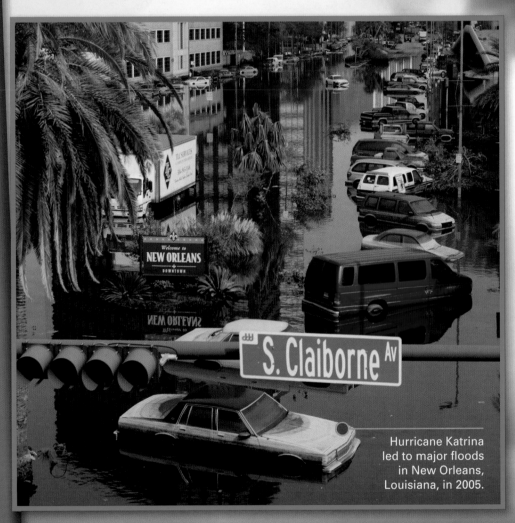

Hurricane Katrina led to major floods in New Orleans, Louisiana, in 2005.

Ten Costliest U.S. Tornadoes

Rank	Location	Year	Damage (in U.S. dollars)
1	Omaha, NE	1975	$1.1 billion
2	Wichita Falls, TX	1979	$840 million
3	Lubbock, TX	1970	$530 million
4	Topeka, KS	1966	$470 million
5	Windsor Locks, CT	1979	$420 million
6	North-central GA	1973	$388 million
7	Xenia, OH	1974	$310 million
8	Grand Island, NE	1980	$260 million
9	St. Louis, MO	1896	$201 million
10	Plainfield, IL	1990	$192 million

Source: NOAA

TORNADO WATCH

Scientists also predict more severe tornadoes. Tornadoes are turning bands of high-speed wind. They can form at a moment's notice.

Researchers at NASA, the U.S. space agency, are using new computer models to study tornadoes. Their models show that summer storms will grow more intense. This is especially true in the central and eastern parts of the United States, as climate change worsens.

FAST FACT
A funnel cloud is a fast-spinning column of water droplets and air. The cone-shaped funnel extends downward from a storm cloud.

A man digs out his car after a record snowfall in Chicago, Illinois.

SNOWBOUND

Chicago, January 2, 1999: The snow kept falling, and falling, and falling. A total of 18.6 inches (47.2 cm) fell in one day. That was a record! A snowstorm struck the Midwest, cutting power, stopping traffic, and closing airports. More than 500,000 people were without electricity for a week.

DEEP FREEZE

Then a deep freeze chilled the region. Temperatures dropped to 0 degrees F (-17 degrees C). In parts of Illinois, thermometers showed readings as low as -36 degrees F (-38 degrees C).

Most people associate global warming with heat. Yet climate change also means that entire regions can turn into a giant ice rink. Each year, 100 major snowstorms blanket the lower United States. Each storm lasts an average of two to five days.

CHINA ON ICE

The more blizzards there are, the more devastation occurs. Blizzards are severe snowstorms with heavy snowdrifts and cold temperatures. Such storms strain the services of communities. These storms can also kill people. In 2008, China had the worst winter in 50 years. Blizzards there killed more than 100 people. The storms shut down parts of China's power supply and transportation system.

Unusually severe snow and ice storms brought China to a near standstill in January 2008.

TURNING UP THE HEAT

In 2003, a killer heat wave fried Europe. Thirty thousand people died over 10 sweltering days. In that same year, a 27-day run of horrible heat killed 2,000 people in India. Such heat waves are becoming more frequent.

Where is the heat coming from? Several recent studies suggest that human-produced emissions of heat-trapping gases are responsible.

Paul Della-Marta is a Swiss scientist. He determined that the length of European heat waves doubled since 1880. In addition, the number of unusually hot days tripled.

These and other studies have many people worried. Joel D. Scheraga works with the Environmental Protection Agency. He estimates that the number of Americans dying from extreme heat and cold could triple by 2050.

Several studies suggest that global warming is making heat waves more severe.

FUELING THE FIRE

A recent increase in wildfires may be the result of record-warm weather and earlier springs. Since the late 1970s, the number of wildfires has gone up. The total area burned has increased, too. Drier, hotter conditions raise the risk of wildfires.

Climate change is linked to an increase in the number and extent of wildfires.

A Rare Twister

During the summer, the streets of New York City can be blistering hot. In 2007, however, summertime brought something unusual. A tornado blew in.

When the tornado touched down, it ripped trees from the ground. The wind peeled back the roofs on buildings. The storm destroyed homes and businesses and knocked out subway service in some areas.

Tornadoes are rare in New York—or at least, they used to be. The 2007 tornado was only the sixth tornado to roll through town since 1950.

Chapter 5

Stopping the Meltdown

Is our planet doomed? Not if we can help it! Many people are working to stop global warming before it gets worse. They believe we can save Earth.

FOSSIL FUEL ADDICTION

Climatologists say humans must stop releasing greenhouse gases into the atmosphere. The world is addicted to fossil fuels. Breaking our dependence will not be easy. People use fossil fuels to run factories and power automobiles. The fuels heat and cool our buildings. In 2007, coal-burning power plants produced more than half of the electricity in the United States. It will not be a simple matter to stop using fossil fuels. Yet some alternative ideas already exist, and more are on the way.

Sunscreen for the Planet?

One Nobel Prize-winning scientist has come up with a different way of cooling Earth. Paul Crutzen suggests launching tiny particles of pollution called **sulfates** into the air. That could block the Sun's rays. This is much like putting sunscreen on your arm.

Another scientist, Tom Wigley, wants airplanes to release sulfates high in the atmosphere. He believes Earth's temperature might decrease by about 9 degrees F (5 degrees C) in a few years.

Other scientists say they don't know whether sulfates will affect the environment and people. They suggest that people reduce their reliance on fossil fuels.

The sulfates block some of the energy from the Sun. **2**

3 Greenhouse gases trap less energy. The atmosphere cools.

Airplanes **1** spray sulfate particles high in the sky.

Sulfates remain in the atmosphere for a few years. Then they need to be added again. **4**

Absorbed Blocked

Will adding particles of pollution to the air bring down Earth's temperature?

These turbines use the wind's energy to make electricity. Wind power can cut our dependence on fossil fuels.

ALTERNATIVE FUELS

Alternative sources of energy can reduce the use of fossil fuels. Those sources include the wind, the Sun, moving water, and heat from within Earth.

Many companies are using wind power to make electricity. A wind farm with 50 windmills can generate 100 megawatts of electricity. That's enough power to light 24,000 homes.

Solar energy is another kind of **renewable energy**. A collection of solar cells, called a solar array, collects and stores energy from the Sun. That energy generates electricity.

Geothermal energy is heat energy that comes from inside Earth. Icelanders use geothermal heat to boil freshwater. The steam turns turbines, which are engines run by turning blades. The turbines make electricity. Running water provides energy, too. That is the basis of **hydropower**.

CARS OF THE FUTURE

Cars of the future might run on electricity from a battery or grease from a deep fryer. Many carmakers are already selling **hybrid vehicles**. Hybrids are cars and trucks that can run on either electricity or gasoline. They use less gas. Hybrid cars are also cleaner, because they produce less pollution.

Some carmakers are experimenting with hydrogen as a power source. Hydrogen is the most abundant element in the universe. How does a hydrogen car work? The car has a hydrogen fuel cell, which is similar to a battery. Inside the fuel cell, hydrogen reacts with oxygen to create electricity. The electricity powers the motor.

It won't be long before you see cars powered by cooking grease. Several companies already sell kits that convert cars into grease-powered vehicles. The grease comes from restaurants.

WHAT DO YOU THINK?

What other sources of energy might replace fossil fuels?

Don't be "shocked" to see electric cars on the roads! Electric power is a clean alternative to gasoline.

KYOTO AND BEYOND

In recent years, many nations have decided to try to control greenhouse gas emissions. In 1997, 150 countries met in Kyoto, Japan. There, they wrote a treaty to reduce greenhouse gases.

The Kyoto agreement went into effect in 2005. So far, 181 countries have agreed to its terms. The United States has refused. U.S. officials say there are problems with the promises they would have to make.

TAKING ACTION

Many U.S. states and local communities are taking steps to cut emissions on their own. They are using the Kyoto treaty as their standard.

Most experts say that when it comes to global warming, inaction is not an option. Everyone must do his or her part.

Kids can take an active role in fighting global warming.

How You Can Help

Here are five easy ways you and your friends can help fight global warming. Can you think of more?

- Turn off the lights, computer, and television when you are not using them.

- Take shorter showers. By heating less water, you will cut energy use.

- Recycle cans, bottles, newspapers, and plastic bags. By recycling, you will cut down on the amount of trash, which helps the environment.

- Plant a tree. Trees clean the air of carbon dioxide while adding oxygen to the environment.

- Ride a bike or walk instead of riding in a car.

It is up to us to help find ways to protect our planet.

SCIENCE AT WORK

CLIMATOLOGIST

Job Description: Climatologists, or atmospheric scientists, identify and interpret climate trends while trying to understand past weather conditions. They also attempt to analyze the current weather conditions.

Job Outlook: Employment is expected to increase.
Earnings: $55,530 to $119,799, with a median income of $77,150

Source: Bureau of Labor Statistics

Conversation With a Climatologist

David H. Bromwich is a climatologist at the Polar Meteorology Group, Byrd Polar Research Center, Ohio State University. He studies global warming and has traveled to Antarctica.

WHAT DO YOU DO?

An atmospheric scientist studies the long-term behavior of the atmosphere over weeks, months, years, decades, and beyond.

WHAT DO YOU LIKE ABOUT THE WORK?

I like that it deals with practical issues that impact the lives of many people. Global warming is an obvious example. Another example is our work with weather forecast models that we have adapted for use in the polar regions. The forecasts are important for those traveling to and from Antarctica each year.

WHAT WAS YOUR TRAINING?

I studied **physics**, mathematics, **meteorology**, and computer science.

WHAT WAS IT LIKE TO WORK IN ANTARCTICA?

It is cold and remote. It is also a privilege because only a small number of people get to be involved. The scenery is spectacular, especially where there are mountains.

WHAT ADVICE DO YOU HAVE FOR STUDENTS INTERESTED IN THIS CAREER?

It is a tremendous field with many opportunities and numerous practical applications. Good physical science abilities are required, so it is good to emphasize these subjects in school.

FIND OUT MORE

BOOKS

Gore, Al. *An Inconvenient Truth: The Crisis of Global Warming, Adapted for a New Generation.* New York: Viking, 2007.

Solway, Andrew. *Fossil Fuels* (Energy for the Future and Global Warming). Pleasantville, NY: Gareth Stevens Publishing, 2008.

Thornhill, Jan. *This Is My Planet: The Kids' Guide to Global Warming.* Toronto: Maple Tree Press, 2007.

WEB SITES

The Big Green Help
**www.nick.com/minisites/biggreen/index.jhtml?adfree=true&_
requestid=167142#**
Nickelodeon has created this site to make kids more aware of the environment. It is packed with simple ways to help the planet.

Environmental Protection Agency
www.epa.gov/climatechange/kids/index.html
The Environmental Protection Agency explains global warming and suggests actions young people can take to care for the environment.

Globalwarmingkids.net
www.globalwarmingkids.net
Find games, activities, and loads of information on climate change at this kid-friendly site.

Publisher's note to educators and parents: Our editors have carefully reviewed these web sites to ensure that they are suitable for children. Many web sites change frequently, however, and we cannot guarantee that a site's future contents will continue to meet our high standards of quality and educational value. Be advised that children should be closely supervised whenever they access the Internet.

GLOSSARY

atmosphere: the envelope of gases around Earth or other space bodies

carbon cycle: the exchange of carbon between living things and the environment

carbon dioxide: one of the gases in the atmosphere; formed when a carbon-based fuel is burned

climatologists: scientists who study the world's climate

compounds: chemical substances made up of two or more elements

condensation: moisture created by cooling or pressure

droughts: times of rain shortage

ecosystem: a community of living organisms

El Niño: a huge area of warm water that appears when winds warm the Pacific Ocean, disrupting global weather patterns

emissions: substances discharged into the air

epidemics: sudden outbreaks of disease in many members of a community at once

evaporation: the process by which a liquid, such as water, turns into a gas

fossil fuels: carbon-based fuels, such as oil and coal, formed by the fossilized remains of plants and animals over millions of years

geothermal energy: energy that comes from the heat in Earth's interior

glaciers: large masses of compacted ice and snow

global warming: the overall warming of Earth's surface over time

greenhouse effect: Earth's warming as carbon dioxide and other gases trap heat near Earth's surface

greenhouse gases: gases that contribute to global warming

habitat: the environment in which an organism lives

hybrid vehicles: cars and trucks that use two or more power sources

hydropower: power generated by moving water

ice age: a period of intense cold and formation of glaciers in Earth's history

krill: tiny shrimplike sea creatures

La Niña: a huge area of cold water that appears when winds cool the Pacific Ocean

meteorology: the study of the atmosphere so weather can be accurately predicted

methane: a colorless, odorless gas that is a component of natural gas

migration: the movement of animals from one place to another for feeding or breeding

physics: the study of the structure of the universe and the properties of matter and energy

plankton: microscopic plant and animal life in the upper layers of freshwater and salt water

precipitation: any form of water that falls to Earth

radiation: energy from a source, such as the Sun, that travels through matter and space

renewable energy: energy from sources that cannot be used up, such as the Sun and wind

sediments: matter that settles to the bottom of a liquid

species: a distinct kind or class of organisms

sulfates: chemical compounds linked to salt

tundra: the treeless area between the ice cap and the trees in the Arctic

INDEX

About the Author

John Perritano is an award-winning journalist who has written about science and the environment for various newspapers, magazines, and web sites. He is the author of many nonfiction titles for children. John holds a master's degree in U.S. history from Western Connecticut State University. John writes from Southbury, Connecticut, where he lives with his three dogs, three cats, and three frogs.